Why this Book?

AUDUBON. "Birds". American. 19th cent.

We are very young when we first become aware of the world of pictures, at which we stare with the same interest whether they are good or bad. The importance of these first long looks is both lasting and considerable.

The only art you will probably have known up till now are the illustrations in your school books, where the pictures are added merely to clarify the lessons; the names of the artists are slipped in by stealth, you might almost say, after the lists of battles, the tables of economic events, and the notes on social life. Of course there are the occasions when you are told by your teacher to study some "art" book at home, or are taken in a bus to the gallery or museum; but the less said about these the better! All the same, your eyes are young and inquisitive, easily impressed and always ready to open in wonder.

It was this realization that led to the idea of compiling the present book—a friendly book, to which you will be able to return again and again; a book in which your eyes will constantly be finding new sources of pleasure, and which has been carefully arranged to guide you, almost without your knowing it, toward the power of distinguishing good from bad. Without forsaking the things that are familiar to you, you will look with fresh eyes at animals, friends, the pleasures of home, the attractiveness of a bunch of flowers or a beautiful piece of furniture. You will see the whole of life set out before you: its joys, its thrills, its daily pageant, its fancies; and by the time you reach the end you will have taken a step on the road to understanding works of art.

There are not many words printed on the picture pages, in order that you may be free to study each illustration without distraction, in all its vividness. For those of you who want to find out more—about the artists, about materials and methods, about the technical terms you will find used here and there—some brief answers are given in the Illustrated Guide that forms the last part of the book.

And now start to turn over the pages, slowly, learning just by using your eyes the enchantment that lies in pictures.

Endpaper pages 2–3. Fresco from the tomb of Nebamon (Egypt)

pierre belvès
françois mathey

enjoying the world of art

AUDUBON. "Birds". American. 19th cent.

"The Little Horses of Lascaux". French. Prehistoric

Printed in Germany · Mohn & Co GmbH, Gütersloh

© Gautier-Languereau, 1965
American edition Gautier-Languereau
and Lion Press Inc. 1966
Library of Congress No. AC 66-10866.

Animal Friends

Many thousands of years ago the first men in the world lived in caves, on the walls of which they drew horses, bison, and mammoths. They didn't do this just for amusement or decoration, but because they thought that by painting pictures of these animals they were making it easier to hunt them; in other words, they invested the pictures with magic powers. Of this we are reasonably certain because many of the paintings (though not the ones shown here) depict the beasts with spears sticking into them. Without successful hunting, men and women would have had neither meat to eat nor skins to wear, and perhaps it was because of this that they took such care to make the "magic" pictures lifelike. At any rate, they certainly did so, not only getting the shapes and colors remarkably correct, but marvelously suggesting the animals' movements and speed. Our wonder becomes still greater when we remember the scanty materials—and learning—available at the time. (See page 91 for some details.)

"The Farmer's Wife". Egypt. 2000 BC. *Painted wood carving*

Mori SOSEN "Young Monkey and Its Mother". Japan. 19th cent. *Painting*

"The Two Geese". Egypt. 2700 BC. *Painting*

"Sheep". (Detail from "The Lady with the Unicorn".) France. 15th cent. *Tapestry*

Albrecht DURER. "Young Hare". German. 1502. *Watercolor*

Pablo PICASSO.
"The Cock".
Spanish. 1938

Katsushika HOKUSAI. "Fishes". Japanese. 19th cent. *Print*

Katsushika HOKUSAI. "Foal and its Mother". *Print*

"Cat". Mexico. *Terracotta*.

"Hippopotamus". Egypt. About 1800 B.C. *Earthenware*

Pai-Shih CHI. "Shrimps". Chinese. 19th cent. *Wash drawing*

"Llama". Peru. *Painted ceramic (pottery).*

Antonio PISANELLO. "Deer". Italian. 15th cent. *Red chalk*

Lin MA. "Birds and Plum Blossom" China. 13th cent. *Painting*

"Abyssinian Zebra". Indian. AD 1621. *Painting*

"Elephant". Persian. 15th cent. *Miniature*

Eugène DELACROIX. "Young Tiger Playing with Its Mother". French. 19th cent. *Lithograph*

REMBRANDT van Rijn. "Lion Resting". Dutch. 17th cent. *Pen drawing*

Animal Figures for Practical Uses

Many real animals are domesticated; so, too, many model animals are made in the form of jugs, door-knockers, or—most popular of all—toys. Here are a few examples from different countries and centuries.

1. NORWAY. Beer mug in form of a hen.
2. GREECE. Perfume container resembling a screech owl.
3. EGYPT. Rouge pot shaped like a grasshopper.
4. ASIA MINOR. Bull zebu (a kind of humped ox)—a wheeled toy.
5. INDIA. Horned animal—also a toy; notice the pivoted head with cord for making it nod.
6. ASIA MINOR. Bird.
7. JAPAN. Tiger—a toy of today.

Louis LE NAIN. "Child Playing a Pipe".
French. 17th cent.

Familiar Portraits

There are really two kinds of pictures of human beings. There is the portrait of a particular person, generally commissioned by him or her in much the same way that we now arrange to be photographed (though painted portraits are also commissioned today—by those who can afford them!); and there is the study of someone, often much too poor or modest to dream of commissioning a picture, who is painted because the artist is interested in his face or something he is doing. The sitter need not be good-looking: usually it is character rather than beauty that the painter seeks, although sometimes, as in Vermeer's very famous portrait of a Dutch girl on the right, he finds both. It is interesting to think that many a man and woman, boy and girl, whose humdrum lives were no different from those of millions and whose very names are lost to us, have through the chance interest of a gifted artist become more familiar to our eyes than the faces of kings and queens or national heroes.

Jan VERMEER
"Young Girl in a Turban"
Dutch. 17th cent.

Mary CASSATT. "Woman Sewing". American. 19th cent.

Pablo PICASSO. "Portrait of Paulo". Spanish. 20th cent.

Amedeo MODIGLIANI. "The Little Girl in Blue". Italian. 20th cent.

Friendly Faces

At some time you have probably heard adults say they wish they could "put the clock back" and become children again. Artists who paint children know of this widespread feeling—indeed, many of them share it—and they know the reason for it, which is that although children have their own worries and sorrows, they have yet to learn about the sort of anxieties and evil things that sadden their elders. So an artist portraying a child will do his best to express this "innocence", this inexperience, in the child's face. It is not easy to say just what makes up such a quality; and therefore only artists who really understand children manage to portray it.

Jean CLOUET. "The French Dauphin" (heir to the throne). French. 16th cent.

Princes and Princesses

Until near the beginning of the present century children were treated as miniature copies of adults—and were dressed like them too! Among the poor this may not have been very conspicuous, but with the elaborate dress of the rich it produced results that we today can only find most odd and "unnatural". Here are three examples from court life.

Antonio MORO. "Alexander Farnese at the Age of Twelve". Dutch. 16th cent.

Diego Rodriguez de Silva y VELASQUEZ. "The Maids of Honor". Spanish. 17th cent.

The story goes that Gainsborough painted this celebrated picture to give the lie to his fellow-portraitist and great rival Sir Joshua Reynolds, who had told a group of students that blue should never be used in large masses in a painting. Whatever the truth of the anecdote, we can readily believe that here is a portrait in which the artist was less concerned, for once, with the character of his subject than with his clothes. Every fold and wrinkle, every shadow and highlight of the blue suit has been painted with the aim of making us feel the very texture of the material.

Thomas GAINSBOROUGH.
"The Blue Boy".
English. 18th cent.

James WHISTLER.
"Portrait of Miss Cicely Alexander".
American. 19th cent.

Marten DE VOS. "Family Portrait". Flemish. 16th cent.

Family Portraits

The fascination of a family portrait lies very often in the details. The children hold toys or cuddle pets, and there is generally a table or chest with small everyday objects on it that provide us with clues for imagining something of what life must have been like in such a household. In the best family portraits, too, you will learn to notice how skilfully the artist has marshalled his figures to make a balanced, pleasing composition without destroying the apparent naturalness of the grouping.

Georges DE LA TOUR. "The Nativity" French. 17th cent.

Mother Love

Mother and child have always been a favorite subject for art. First and foremost come the Madonna and the Infant Jesus; and above you will see them depicted, rather unusually, like any humble young mother and baby living in the artist's own day. But the attraction of painting parenthood has drawn artists of many beliefs and civilizations, as the Japanese print on the right makes evident.

Kitagawa UTAMARO. "Mother and Child". Japanese. 18th cent. *Print*.

Edouard MANET. "The House at Rueil". French. 19th cent.

Claude MONET. "The Artist's Garden at Giverny". French. 19th cent.

The Charm of Home

Pictures of houses and gardens offer the artist different problems from portraits of people and animals. Here there is no question of penetrating the character concealed in a face, catching a child's mood, investing an animal with grace and movement. A picture that principally shows plants or non-living things, like a house or objects on a table, depends for its success on how the artist decides to present his subject, his choice of colors, and his method of applying them. When *you* draw a house you probably draw it all. But the interest of Manet's picture, above, lies in his having chosen to show only part of the frontage, with a tree trunk almost hiding the front door. Monet's garden, too, would look much less interesting without the path dividing up the mass of flowers.

Pierre BONNA[RD]
"The Dining Roo[m]"
French. 20th ce[nt.]

Jan BRUEGHEL. "Flowers".
Flemish. 17th cent.

Flowers and Fruit

Flowers, fruit, stuffed birds, fish on a plate—all these are known in art as "Still Life". You can probably think of other subjects that come under the same heading. In looking at paintings of cut flowers, don't ignore the vase. The artist has in most cases devoted just as much care to it as to the blooms, and sometimes it is the most effective part of the picture.

Paul CÉZAN
"Apples and Orange
French. 19th ce

Frans SNYDERS. "A Fruit Seller". Flemish. 17th cent.

Pieter BRUEGHEL the Elder. "Wedding Dance". Flemish. 16th cent.

Scenes from Life

Many painters have taken pleasure in recording typical events in the life around them; and for us who come after, such scenes form as valuable a historical record as any written account. Without these artists we should have no detailed or accurate knowledge of how ordinary people dressed, and only a vague idea of their customs and recreations.

David TENIERS the Youn[ger]
"The Village F[...]
Flemish. 17th c[...]

Jacob JORDAENS.
"The King Drinks".
Flemish. 17th cent.

High Days and Holidays

Weddings, festivals, fairs, domestic celebrations: such occasions for getting together and being happy have always appealed to painters, even more than the happenings of every day. For one thing, these are the times when people forget their shyness, the stuck-up ones come down to earth, and all of us temporarily become friendly equals. Secondly, the artist can show the different ways in which people of different ages and temperaments behave in a situation that is common to them all; and finally, such assemblies give him fine technical opportunities in the arrangement of groups, colors, and light and shadow.

Jan STE
"The Feast of St. Nicho
Dutch. 17th c

Pieter BRUEGHEL the Elder. "Battle Between Carnival and Lent." Flemish. 16th cent.

Jérôme (or Hieronymus) BOSCH. "The Conjurer". Dutch. 15th cent.

Strolling Down the Street

A point to be remembered about the sort of scene we have been dealing with in the last few pages is that here are no models, prepared to sit patiently for the artist, but people unaware that they are being painted, and constantly changing position. The artist can therefore make only lightning sketches to prompt his imagination when he gets back to the studio.

Louis-Léop
BOIL
"The Stag
French. 19th ce

Jean TASSEL. "The Carpenters". French. 17th cent.

Jan VERMEER. "The Lacemakers". Dutch. 17th cent.

Gustave COURBET. "The Winnowers". French. 19th cent.

Marcel GROMAIRE. "The Flemish Reaper". French. 20th cent.

At Work

We have already noted the debt historians owe to artists for accurate information about old customs, pastimes, and styles of dress. Pictures are an equally vital source of information about methods of work in bygone times, particularly before the invention of the camera. If you are tempted to feel that some commonplace occupation is a strange subject to inspire a masterpiece, remember that the painter too is a worker; his art is no casual amusement, but a craft to be painstakingly learned and then carried on in long spells of hard toil. People do paint in their spare time—maybe you do, or will; but those who limit it to this very rarely become great masters.

Frans SNYDERS (attributed to). "The Fruit Merchant". Flemish. 17th cent.

Louis LE NAIN. "The Forge". French. 17th cent.

Fernand LÉGER. "The Builders". French. 20th cent.

Théodore GÉRICAULT.
"Light Cavalry Officer of the Imperial Guard".
French. 19th cent.

Action Pictures

Movement, speed, energy, physical strength—these are the qualities that appeal to the painter of action pictures. It is not easy to make a still image appear to be in motion. To do so successfully the artist must learn a great deal about the anatomy of the human body and of whatever creatures he intends to paint; that is to say, about the structure of their bones, the size and position of each muscle, where fat covers the muscles, and so on. And having mastered all this, he must go on to study what happens to all the parts with every kind of movement. Otherwise his subject will not seem to be in motion at all, but remain clumsy and 'wooden'.

Eugène DELACRO
"Knights in Combat in Open Countr
French. 19th ce

"Alexander and Darius in Combat".
Roman. *Mosaic*.

Albrecht ALTDORFER.
"Alexander at the Battle of Arbela".
German. 16th cent.

(An enlarged portion of this tiny but crowded painting, showing Alexander's opponent Darius, is shown on left)

On pages 58 and 59:

Paolo UCCELLO.
"The Rout of San Romano".
Italian. 15th cent.

Eugène ISABEY.
"Jean Bart at the Battle of Texel".
French. 19th cent.

Sea Pictures

Here is movement of another kind, created by the tireless sea and the invisible wind. Battles at sea have always had a special fascination for marine artists, perhaps because of the challenge to their skill presented by all the different types of motion involved: the surge of the waves, the flying spray, the rolling of the ships, the flapping of sails and ensigns, the smoke rising from guns and burning timbers. Water also offers the painter the problem of how to make it look genuinely wet. This arises particularly with pictures of smooth seas or placid lakes and rivers.

William TURNER.
"The Battle of Trafalgar".
English. 19th cent.

Willem VAN DER VELDE the Younger. "The Cannon Shot". Dutch. 17th cent.

65

Antony VAN DYCK (or VANDYKE) "Portrait of Charles I of England" Flemish. 17th cent.

Jacques Louis DAVID. "The Coronation of Napoleon I". French. 19th cent.

Historical Painters

As we have seen, any artist in past times who faithfully depicted the life that went on around him has become a historical painter for later generations. Other artists served history more strictly by painting the likenesses of the famous or commemorating great events. Others again, drew on their imaginations to bring to life great happenings of which no contemporary picture has come down to us.

Until a century or two ago artists depicting scenes from the Bible always endowed them with the architecture and fashions of the painter's own day. This picture is part of a much larger one covering the walls of a princely family's private chapel in Florence, and although it is supposed to illustrate a Bible story it really shows a contemporary procession, including, we may be reasonably sure, recognizable portraits of most of the members of the family!

Benozzo GOZZOLI
"Journey of the Magi to Bethlehem".
Italian. 15th cent.

Gentile DA FABRIANO. "The Adoration of the Magi". Italian. 15th cent.

Raoul DUFY.
"The Red Violin".
French. 20th cent.

Art and Music

To the other things of which artists throughout the centuries have unintentionally given us the history, may be added musical instruments. If you have ever explored old churches you will very likely have seen medieval instruments, and their players, carved in the stonework and on the ends of the pews. Here are two pictures showing that in our own century painters are still interested in the visual aspects of the sister-art.

"The Dancer in the Salmon-colored Skirt"

"The Pas Battu" (a ballet step)

"Dancer on the stage"

Edgar DEGAS.
French. 19th cent.

The Pleasures of the Dance

The graceful agility of the ballet dancer has, not unnaturally, appealed to a succession of artists during the last hundred years or so, but to none with such brilliant results as to the Frenchman Edgar Dégas. For some of his pictures he did not use paint, but pastel, with which he caught the intensity of the reflected footlights so remarkably that the dancers themselves seem luminous. In other pictures he studied the dancers behind the scenes, revealing them as no longer fairylike nymphs, but hard-working, tired women.

"Dancers Behind the Scenes"

"Two Dancers"

Edouard VUILLARD. "The Imaginary Invalid". French. 20th cent.

The theatre has attracted artists in three ways: as designers of scenery, as recorders of plays in the course of being performed, and as painters of the players behind the scenes, just as Dégas liked to paint ballet dancers behind the scenes. Above is a modern picture of a scene in one of the world's most famous classical comedies, *Le Malade Imaginaire*—"The Man Who Thought He Was Ill"—by Molière, the great 17th-century actor-dramatist. Georges Seurat, who painted the circus picture, was one of a group of French artists who did much for our enjoyment by exploring new techniques.

Theatre and Circus

Georges SEURAT.
"The Circus".
French. 19th cent.

Henri de TOULOUSE-LAUTREC.
"The Jockey".
French. 19th cent.

Art and Sport

Toulouse-Lautrec, celebrated for his posters and music-hall pictures, also delighted in horses although he was too badly deformed to ride. The two modern pictures were painted by artists less interested in realism than in the play of the swiftly moving patches of color on a sports field.

Robert DELAUNAY. "The Runners". French. 20th cent.

Henri MATISSE.
"Open window at Collioure"
(a tiny port at the Mediterranean end
of the Pyrenees).
French. 20th cent.

Holiday Scenes

Going away for a holiday is quite a recent form of relaxation. Before the coming of railways the well-to-do traveled only to visit friends or improve their education, and the poor hardly traveled at all. Even when people did start going to the seashore, it was mainly because they thought sea-bathing had great medicinal properties. Paintings of holiday scenes (as distinct from merry-making at home) therefore go back little more than a hundred years, and the habit of sketching (or photographing) beauty spots while on holiday is more recent still. Appreciation of natural beauty has increased enormously in the last 200 years; before that no artist would consider painting a landscape unless it "told a story" with human figures in it.

Claude MONET.
"Yachts at Argenteuil".
(on the river Seine).
French. 19th cent.

Raoul DUFY. "Riders in a Wood". French. 20th c

English countryside:

John CONSTABLE.
"Dedham Mill" (Essex).
English. 19th cent.

The clear light of Tuscany (central Italy):

Jean-Baptiste Camille COROT.
"Florence Seen from the Boboli Gardens".
French. 19th cent.

On Tahiti (south Pacific):

Paul GAUGUIN.
"Riders on the Shore".
French. 19th cent.

In China:

WANG Meng.
"Mountain in Autumn".
Chinese. 14th cent. (Yuan Dynasty)

Henri ROUSSEAU ('The Douanier Rousseau'). "Old Juniet's Trap". French. 19th cent.

The Outing

About the beginning of this century, influenced largely by the strange work of Gauguin in Tahiti, artists became interested in a return to much simpler styles. One of the most striking of the new school was Henri Rousseau, nicknamed from his occupation "The Customs Man". Rousseau was a genuine "primitive", knowing next to nothing of the rules of art; yet, as the above amusing group shows, his pictures were unusual and oddly impressive. Compare this with Pissarro's vastly different style in the exquisite painting opposite.

Camille PISSARR
"Approach
the Village
French. 19th ce

Henri MATISSE. "The King's Sorrow". French. 20th cent.

The painters in this book should by now have become your friends forever. Each time you come back to them it will, we hope, be with pleasure.

One skims through a magazine, reads a book of adventure, but comes back again and again to a book on Art. Why not turn a corner of your room into your own private Art Gallery? Along with your stamp album, holiday snapshots, and those mysterious stones and shells one brings home from the shore, start a collection of reproductions of paintings that appeal to you. You'll be surprised how often they appear in magazines and even newspapers, and if you find the going a bit difficult at first, your parents or your teacher will surely be ready with helpful suggestions.

But perhaps our artists have inspired you with an urge to draw for yourself? As a start, choose one of the pictures and try copying—not tracing—it in pencil. Very likely you'll be appalled by the result, but you'll be amazed to find how many details in the original had hitherto escaped your notice. And even if you feel it's going to be a great deal harder than you had thought to learn how to draw well, you'll already have discovered a new way of "looking" and enjoying.

From copying to drawing from the real thing is only a step, and doubtless you'll be impatient to make it. Whatever you do, don't say "I haven't got the gift", for it isn't true. We can all express ourselves, and what matters is not whether you are clever at it, but whether you are honest with yourself, doing the best you can and developing your own way of looking at things. Even an unskilled hand can lead you into an enchanted world of the imagination. Off, then, to your paintbrushes!

Pierre-Auguste RENOIR.
"Jean Renoir Drawing".
French. 19th cent.

ILLUSTRATED GUIDE

Pages 2–3

Fresco from the Tomb of
NEBAMON
Egypt. 15th cent. B.C.
Thebes, Upper Egypt

FRESCO. A form of wall decoration in which the picture is painted direct on to damp or "fresh" plaster. ("Fresco" is Italian for "fresh".)

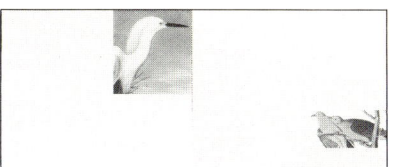

Pages 4–5

John James AUDUBON
1780–1851, American
"Birds"

A naturalist has a duty to depict exactly what he sees. But if he is to create a work of art, something more is needed. And that is just what we find in the astonishing work of James Audubon. Talented craftsmanship, perfect knowledge of the animal world, an urge to give life to his pictures. . . . In America the name Audubon is synonymous with the study and love of nature.

Pages 6–7

"The Little Horses of Lascaux". France.
20,000 to 30,000 years old.
Cave of Lascaux, Dordogne region, S.W. France

This historic cavern was discovered in 1940 by some boys whose dog had fallen through a hole in the ground.
The little horses form part of a large painted area on which bison and reindeer can also be seen. The pictures are at least 20,000 years old, some think much older.
ROCK PAINTINGS. Yellow ochre, red iron ore, and black manganese oxide were ground up and mixed with animal fat: these were the materials with which the prehistoric artist went so cleverly to work, using his fingers as a brush or sometimes filling a hollow bone with color.

France: *Font-de-Gaume, Les Eyzies, Les Combarelles*
Spain: *Altamira, Gasulla Gorge, Cogul, Alpera*

Page 8

"The Farmer's Wife". Egypt. 2000 B.C.
Hildesheim Museum, Germany

A familiar scene throughout Man's history—a farmer's wife with a cow and calf. The group, in beautifully carved wood, appears to have been a toy. Its owner must have loved it, since he chose it to accompany him into the next world as a reminder of his life in this one.
POLYCHROMY. The word means decorating with many colors. The wood was cut to shape, covered with liquid plaster, and then the artist did the rest.

Page 9

Mori SOSEN 1749–1821, Japanese
"Young Monkey and Its Mother".
Vever Collection, Paris

Thoughtful mother, inattentive child—the story of all motherhood, told us by these charming little Japanese monkeys.
This painting, which portrays its subject so sensitively, is nearly 200 years old, yet it could have come from a modern sketchbook.

Page 10

"Geese" from the Tomb of Itet at Meidum
Egypt. 2700 B.C.
Cairo Museum

Waddling like all geese since geese began, two by two, you could believe they had been painted only yesterday. In fact, they are well over 4000 years old! With others like them they formed a frieze—that is to say, a decorative strip along the top of the walls—in the corridor of a tomb. Today they are admired by visitors to Cairo's fine Museum.
"Hunting and Fishing", *British Museum*

Page 11

"Sheep"—part of "The Lady with the Unicorn" tapestry. France. About 1495.
Cluny Museum, Paris

In this tapestry an attractive lady is amusing herself with a unicorn; all round her, rabbits, foxes, monkeys, lions and this sheep frisk and frolic, while in between them is a carpet of flowers woven in wool and silk.

TAPESTRY. In the Middle Ages tapestry was primarily a French art, its chief centers being Arras (you may have heard the expression "behind the arras"), Beauvais, and the Gobelins factory in Paris. But before the weaver could begin his part of the work, an artist had to provide a design—although many weavers would make changes of their own as they went along. Fine tapestries were also made at Mortlake, Surrey.
Victoria and Albert Museum, London
Coventry Cathedral

Page 12.

Albrecht DURER 1471–1528, German
"Young Hare" Watercolor
Louvre, Paris

One of the greatest masters of German art, Albrecht (Albert) Dürer is mainly celebrated for his important oil paintings and engravings; but he also executed drawings, watercolors, and gouaches (see below) that demonstrate his love of animals and plants.

WATERCOLOR. A pigment mixed with gum-arabic, honey, or other binding agents that dissolve in water; known in Egypt since the 2nd century A.D.

GOUACHE. Watercolor pigment mixed with white "body" color to make it opaque and non-glossy. Poster paints are gouaches.

Page 13

Pablo PICASSO. Born 1881, Spanish
"The Cock" Pastel, 1938
Ralph F. Colin collection, New York

The cock must have a good claim to be the creature that has inspired artists, down the centuries, to their extremest flights of fancy. Here is Picasso's version, proud, arrogant, fashioned like a piece of architecture.

PASTEL. This is a kind of soft chalk, agreeable and seemingly easy to use. Its range of colors is great, but alas! to keep pastel colors from deteriorating is far from easy. It is not that they fade, but they adhere so lightly that pieces come away at a touch.

Page 14

Katsushika HOKUSAI 1760–1849, Japanese
"Fishes". Print.
Musée Guimet, Paris.

Hokusai well deserves his two appearances in our book. First for the quality of his drawing—witness how "fluid" the two carp look—and secondly for his great kindness to children. A child had only to say he would like, for instance, a painting of his kite, and Hokusai would drop everything—sketches, illustrations, prints—to afford him that pleasure.

Page 15

Katsushika HOKUSAI 1760–1849, Japanese
"Foal and its Mother" Print
National Library, Paris

The delicate and harmonious curves of this drawing give it a special tenderness. Hokusai was a man who lived his long life solely for his art; people called him "mad on it", as people say about any absorbing interest that is not their own.

JAPANESE PRINTS. There were two methods of producing these. In the earlier, the outlines of the work were first traced on to a block of wood, which was then cut away between them, leaving them as ridges. The colored areas were hand-copied through stencils on to sheets of rice paper or silk, and the outlines were added in black by pressing down the woodblock. Later, about 200 years ago, woodblocks began to be used for the colored areas as well, although it meant cutting a separate block for each color. The outlines were added as before.

Page 16

"Cat" Terracotta. Mexico. Modern
San Pedro Tlaquepaque, Mexico

This delightful cat, adorned with flowers like a bouquet, comes from the tiny village of San Pedro Tlaquepaque, or simply Tlaquepaque, in the west-central part of Mexico. The peasants there have two interests: farming and pottery. Whether glazed or matt, their pottery is always decorated with a flower or animal motif, and conceals a surprise—for the soil of the region, from which it is made, is naturally scented!

TERRACOTTA. Clay molded and shaped, then either dried in the sun or baked in an oven. Statuettes, as well as vessels, may be made of terracotta. ("Terra cotta"=cooked earth or clay.)

Page 17

"Hippopotamus" Faience (glazed earthenware)
Egypt. 2000–1785 B.C.
Cairo Museum

His head adorned with a lotus flower, his sides with the papyrus plant from which the ancients made an equivalent of paper, this blue hippopotamus looks as though he has just come out of the water. He is certainly an unusual specimen!

FAIENCE. Two bakings are needed, the first to harden the clay—which up to this point is the same as terracotta—the second to harden and attach the special glazing or enamel, containing tin, which converts the terracotta into faience and gives it its high gloss. The word 'faience' comes from 'Faenza', the Italian town where it used to be made. The Italians themselves call it 'Majolica', a name we also use sometimes.

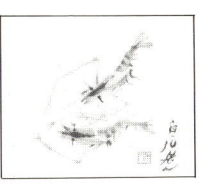

Page 18

CHI Pai-shih 1861–1957. Chinese
"The Shrimps" Wash drawing

Transparent, vivacious, ready to dart away, yet, held prisoner in the shallows . . . The artist is said to have remarked: "It took me six months to study them, one minute to paint them".

WASH-DRAWING. Instead of pigment, a special type of ink is diluted with water and applied with a brush. In this example an added effect has been obtained by using a paper made from straw and bark and resembling blotting paper. When the brush touches it with a drop of ink, the drop spreads out into strange shapes.

Page 19

"Llama" Painted Ceramic. Peru
National Archeological Museum, Lima

With eyes wide and ears erect, this llama in the South American Andes has been surprised on the alert. The Inca huntsman, after having stalked and studied it, made a thing of beauty out of its clay effigy.

PAINTED CERAMIC. The modeled clay is put to bake in the potter's oven. On being taken out it is painted, then baked again. ("Ceramics" is the name given to the potter's art.)

Page 20

Antonio PISANELLO 1395–1455, Italian
"Deer" Red Chalk
Louvre, Paris

The pencil flits to and fro as lightly as a caress, within an outline as clean cut as the profile on a medal.

RED CHALK. Also known as "sanguine", from its resemblance to blood, this chalk produces a soft and beautiful effect that can be of great help to the artist, but it is difficult to use, being impossible to alter or touch up. Sometimes it is employed on tinted paper, when it can be combined (as here) with black and white chalks.
National Gallery, London

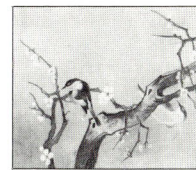

Page 21

MA Lin c. 1190–1260. Chinese (Sung Dynasty
"Birds and Plum Blossom"
Goto Museum, Tokyo

Happy country where the Emperor himself was a painter of genius! Snowy mountains, rivers with waterfalls, starry skies . . . a bird on the branch of a plum tree in flower . . . Every form of life deeply interested the Chinese artist. But don't be misled; the subject is merely a pretext for the painter to indulge his personal fancy. He discovers the harmony in a line, the purity of a hue, or the simple beauty of a facial expression . . . to all of which he brings the perception of a poet. (See Illustrated Guide note to page 83 right.)

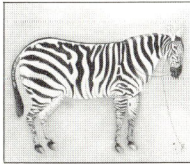

Page 22

"Abyssinian Zebra" Painting. India, 1621
Victoria and Albert Museum, London

The markings of a zebra seem to suggest modern art, yet with this picture we are in India, at the court of Prince Jehangir, more than three centuries ago.

MAKING USE OF BACKGROUND. To draw this zebra the artist has made clever use of the white paper on which he has worked; and the fact that the animal's white stripes are formed by the actual white of the background gives the picture a pleasing unity. Nevertheless, this is a tricky device that requires to be clearly worked out in advance.

Page 23

"Elephant" Miniature. Persia, 15th cent.
Herat, Afghanistan

The elephant moves forward with his slow, ponderous step. His skin, tawny and wrinkled, has been painted with care. In fact the subject is handled to perfection, the details of eye and trunk, particularly, showing nice observation.

MINIATURES. Miniature-painting is a specialized art demanding the greatest precision with every detail. It was developed during the Middle Ages in Europe's abbeys and courts, but the most beautiful, intricate and renowned examples come from Persia, India, and China. During the 17th and 18th centuries miniature portraits were very popular, especially in England.

Page 24

Eugène Delacroix 1798–1863, French
"Young Tiger Playing with Its Mother".
Lithograph
National Library, Paris

It is pleasant to imagine Delacroix temporarily forsaking his huge historical paintings to go and see the lions and tigers in the Paris Zoo. On returning to his studio he would re-create the charming frolics of wild beasts happy to regain an hour of liberty.

LITHOGRAPHY. The drawing is made with a wax pencil on fine limestone or zinc. The stone is then moistened; the waxy markings of course repel the water, which remains only on the blank areas. Next, a fatty ink is spread over the surface, and the opposite result ensues—the ink is held only on the waxy areas, that is, the lines of the picture. The water dries, and it is then possible to print off many duplicates of the drawing.

Page 25

REMBRANDT van Rijn 1606–1669, Dutch
"Lion Resting" Pen Sketch
Louvre, Paris

After his circus act the old lion rests. He no longer has the strength to go on prancing round, and his sorrowful and faraway look ignores the eye fixed upon him.

PEN DRAWING. A goose quill expertly sharpened, a little sepia ink, and the drawing takes shape like so much elegant and flowing handwriting. In his later years, Rembrandt preferred a pen cut from a reed.
Rembrandt drawings:
British Museum, London
Victoria and Albert Museum, London

Pages 26–27

Animal Figures
for Practical Uses

Model animals lend themselves uncomplainingly to all sorts of fantasies, but they still need to be treated with affection and imagination.
Picture the hen-shaped drinking vessel on this page brimming with beer, the screech-owl perfume container and the cleverly designed rouge-pot being used by the ladies of Athens and Thebes respectively as they made up their faces. The toys need even less imagination, for we have their counterparts with us today, like the roaring tiger designed to fill tiny Japanese tots with delicious terror. There must be many more ancient toys, long vanished, that we should find equally familiar.

Page 28

Louis LE NAIN 1593–1648, French
"Child Playing on a Pipe" (part of a larger painting called "The Cart")
Louvre, Paris

You will find this pipe-player in that great Parisian art gallery, the Louvre, which contains one of the three or four best collections of pictures in the world. The larger painting of which this is part shows a hay wagon. The peasant boy is perched on top of the hay, playing to an audience of three little girls. The period is that of King Louis XIII.

Page 29

Jan VERMEER of Delft 1632–1675, Dutch
"Young Girl Wearing a Turban"
Johan Maurits van Nassau Foundation, The Hague

As famous as the Mona Lisa, this turbaned

young girl is among the great pictures that reduce the viewer to silent admiration, though the silence here is one in which it is not hard to imagine yourself hearing the tinkle of a harpsichord or spinet.

Vermeer—his full name was really Van der Meer—was one of the greatest painters of his time, and indeed of all time, in spite of his early death at 43.

Page 30

Left:
Lucas CRANACH 1472–1553, German
"Portrait of a Young Girl"
Louvre, Paris

    One of the finest ways of getting to understand pictures is to compare them. On these two pages you have a chance to compare:
- The quick and supple brush of Rubens
- The mastery of Goya
- The outstanding draftsmanship of Picasso
- The freshness of Mary Cassatt
- The originality of Modigliani

It remains for Cranach to capture the gentle sadness of this young girl's face and to show us the real pleasure he evidently took, despite his severe style, in painting beautiful blonde tresses against a black gown.

Centre:
Peter Paul RUBENS 1577–1640, Flemish
"Portrait of the Artist's Son" (part of a larger portrait of "Helen Fourment and her Children")
Louvre, Paris

Sometimes in the midst of his fame and his many commissions, his activities as painter, art collector, and ambassador, Rubens would slow down the spinning whirlpool of his life for long enough to pay attention to his young wife and children; and it seems to have been during one of these pauses that he created the portrait which includes this charming study of his son Francis at the age of three.

If you ever go to see the picture, in the Louvre, you will also find in the scene the boy's mother, Helen Fourment, and his little sister Clara Joan. For some time Rubens was ambassador for Philip IV of Spain to the court of King Charles I, and it was during this time that he painted the splendid ceiling of the Banqueting Hall in Whitehall.
Ceiling of the Banqueting Hall, Whitehall, London

Right:
Francisco José de GOYA y Lucientes
1746–1828, Spanish "Portrait of Mariano"
The Duke of Albuquerque's collection, Madrid

Goya is one of the masters of the Spanish school of painting and one of the greatest names in art.

He became a painter while hardly out of his teens, and his output during the rest of his long life was enormous; but his talents never declined, and the last portrait he ever finished (a French milkmaid) at the age of 81, shows his touch to be as sure as ever.

His work is a strange mixture of anger and tenderness: anger in his pictures of revolution, executions, and the horrors of war, tenderness in his portraits of people he liked—though he could be merciless in his studies of those he did not!

Mariano, shown here against a dark background that sets off the cheerful expression, was Goya's well-loved grandson.
The Prado, Madrid

In Great Britain there is no large collection of Goyas. The following are some of the galleries in which you may see one or more paintings:
The National Gallery, London. The Wellington Museum, London. The Bowes Museum, Barnard Castle. National Gallery of Scotland, Edinburgh. The Courtauld Institute of Art, London.

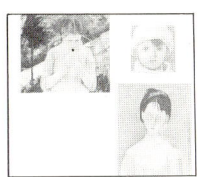

Page 31

Left:
Mary CASSATT 1845–1927, American
"Woman Sewing"
Louvre, Paris

    Born near Pittsburgh, USA, Mary Cassatt went to Paris to complete her art studies. Here she immediately fell under the spell of the "Impressionists" (who were under much adverse criticism at the time) and was welcomed by them as a friend. Sharing a common ideal, she entered into their enthusiasm, felt the drama surrounding them to be hers too, upheld and defended them, and gave them access to all the American collections.
The Art Galleries, Glasgow

Right:
Pablo PICASSO Born 1881, Spanish
"Portrait of Paulo" (1923)
Pablo Picasso collection

When young people in France draw something out of the ordinary, they say 'I've done a Picasso!' Certainly his paintings astonish you, upset your ideas, even repel you; but you have to admit that they never leave you indifferent, and that some of them move you to admiration, such as this beautiful portrait of Paulo at the age of two.

Below:
Amedeo MODIGLIANI 1884–1920, Italian
"The Little Girl in Blue"
Private collection in Paris

A precise line traces out the form of the picture. The colors are restrained and flat, with no attention to light and shadow. The brushwork lacks technical skill. And yet there is nothing wanting in the young girl's serious face. Few artists have made so original a mark in so short a life span as this strange Italian.

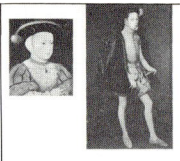

Page 32

Left:
Jean CLOUET 1475–1541, French
"The French Dauphin" (son of François I)
Antwerp Museum

People posed for the Clouets (Jean and François) as they do nowadays for the photographer.

Famous portraitists, well in the fashion favored at the time, they first drew each sitter from life, in pencil. Then the painting was done, with minute attention to finish and detail, on panels of wood, generally quite small.

Right:
Antonio MORO 1519–1576, Dutch
"Alexander Farnese at the Age of Twelve"
Della Pilotta Palace, Parma, Italy

His real name was Antonio Moor van Dashoorst. After being brought up in Holland he traveled widely in Italy, England, Portugal, and Spain, where he became Painter to the King.

The young Prince Farnese, aged 12, is seen here in three-quarter full face pose. Moro has captured admirably the proud elegance of his model, whose family name is among the half-dozen greatest in Italian history.

Page 33

Diego Rodriguez de Silva y VELASQUEZ
1598–1660, Spanish
"The Maids of Honor" (Las Meninas)

Here indeed is one of the peaks of the painter's art. The brush is like a living thing, designing, painting, creating effects of transparency or profound solidity, putting everything exactly in its place. Shadows and highlights merge and blend only to separate again; blacks, fawns, and the delicate touches of pink are poised in perfect equilibrium, even though our reproduction covers only a part of the complete painting in order to be large enough to show details.

You feel you are looking at a real-life incident. Yet practically nothing is happening. The Infanta Margarita, bathed in light, proud and mischievous, offers you the freshness of her glance. Her maids of honor fuss about her. The little girl has come to the studio to watch Velasquez (on the left) paint a portrait of her parents the King and Queen, whose reflections you can see in the mirror. In a moment, you feel, she will drop a curtsy and go away again, followed by her maids and probably the big dog. The incident could belong to today instead of 300 years ago.

Page 34

Thomas GAINSBOROUGH 1727–1788,
English "The Blue Boy"
Huntington collection, San Marino, California, USA

The "dominant" color here is blue, and all the other colors combine to stress the fact: the rose-gray of the sky, the white of the collar, the black of the hair and hat. And in his portrait of this young man, dressed as in the time of Rubens, Gainsborough has given us a real lesson in painting.

DOMINANT COLOR. At times certain painters, either by instinct or deliberately, compose a picture as a harmony of colors centered on, and subordinate to, one *dominant* color.

Page 35

James WHISTLER 1834–1903, American
"Miss Cicely Alexander"
Tate Gallery, London

Some painters choose bright colors, others prefer more subtle harmonies; while others again, like Whistler, are keenest on grays. The gradations of gray are infinite, and go well with white and black. Whistler was an American who spent much of his life in London and Paris.

GRAYS. Black added to white, with a touch of color, gives a tinted gray; rose-gray, beige-gray, and blue-gray all come into this category. A touch of colour mixed into black improves it—and white is white only by contrast with its surroundings: a contrast that depends for its success on the distribution of colors on the canvas.

Page 36

Marten DE VOS 1536–1603, Flemish
"Family Portrait"
Royal Museum of Fine Arts, Brussels

Like many of his contemporaries, Marten de Vos had duly traveled to Italy, visited Rome, and, during a stay in Venice, had worked in the studio of an artist of renown. Back again in Flanders, he decorated churches and public buildings, and in particular painted the portraits of civic worthies. The present group are Antony Anselmo, an Antwerp alderman, his wife Joan Hooffmans, and their children Giles and Joan.

PORTRAITS. Painting portraits is an especially delicate art, since it is necessary both to produce a recognizable likeness and please (which usually means flatter) the sitter. And even this is only the façade behind which the painter must find his own self-expression.

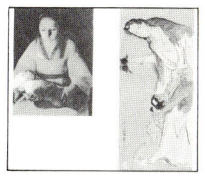

Page 37

Left:
Georges DE LA TOUR 1593–1652, French
"The Nativity" (detail)
Rennes Museum, Brittany

An unusual fate befell the work of this painter from Lorraine. An acknowledged master in his day (one of his paintings hung in Louis XIII's bedroom), he was then forgotten for centuries, his pictures being attributed to other artists or simply lost. Here, a woman holds on her knees a newborn child swaddled with the thoroughness of bygone days. Respect and delicacy characterize her attitude and expression. And the Birth of all births is signalized by an intimate and secret radiance.

Right:
Kitagawa UTAMARO 1753–1806, Japanese
"Mother and Child"
National Museum, Tokyo

We are made to feel decidedly far away by this very different manner of seeing and interpreting life! People in the West during the 19th century felt a similar surprise on first seeing Japanese prints: simple drawings engraved on wood and printed over colors applied through a stencil (see Illustrated Guide note to Page 15). In spite of this rather mechanical method, the mother's face here is filled with tender expression as she plays with her child.

PRINTS AND OLD REPRODUCTIONS. Originally Japanese prints were sold very cheaply; similarly in Europe one needed only a few pence to purchase beautiful copies of popular pictures. Today the former are as eagerly sought after as the latter.

Page 38

Left:
Edouard MANET 1832–1883, French
"House at Rueil"
Orangery of Charlottenburg Palace, Berlin

Manet spent several holidays in this house just outside Paris. The façade reflects the sun, and the painter, without bothering about new techniques, has simply let his brush lead him on. It is summertime, the easel is pretty surely well in the shade, and after a series of studio sessions such a task in the open air must be a real joy.

SKETCH. A painting made direct from nature and not as a "fair copy" later in the studio. It could be called a note in color, a rapid likeness, a fleeting impression that the artist is anxious to seize and make permanent. (See Illustrated Guide note to page 85, 'Impressionism'.)

Right:
Claude MONET 1840–1926, French
"The Painter's Garden at Giverny"
The Bührle collection, Zurich

Claude Monet had a garden at Giverny on the banks of the river Epte, a tributary of the Seine. If he painted his garden, he also tended it, making a pond here, planting trees there, keeping a watchful eye on the color scheme of the flower beds and herbaceous borders. When his scrutiny had satisfied him, when the sun twinkled through the leaves of the willows, when the dragonflies were admiring their reflections in the pool—then he would paint, inviting us to enter this amazing fairyland by means of his canvas.

Page 39

Pierre BONNARD 1867–1947, French
"The Dining Room Overlooking the Garden"
Guggenheim Museum, New York

Bonnard's sensitive vision converted everything into a posy of vivid colors. His compositions are built up of light strokes, featherweight touches. His color is never laid on in thick masses. Everything is like a whisper, a collection of subtle vibrations. Blues, oranges, pinks, mauves; the light floods in from the garden upon all of them, transfiguring fruit and flowers with its summer brilliance.

Page 40

Jan BRUEGHEL ("Velvet Brueghel")
1568–1625, Flemish
"Flowers"
*M.H. de Young Memorial Museum,
San Francisco, USA*
(Gift of Mrs. Herbert Fleischhacker)

What a fine family of painters the Brueghels were! The one represented here, Jan, was nicknamed Velvet Brueghel because of his taste for rich clothes. Painter of garlands, bouquets, bowls of flowers—what pleasanter subjects could you have?

Note with what care he has arranged his bouquet: the most important flower near the center, the colors well varied, a few stems left visible to prevent the floral mass looking too heavy. And have you spotted the beetle on the table and other insects among the blossoms?

FLOWER PAINTERS. Some artists specialize in certain subjects, and there are many ways for a specialist to show a simple bouquet. There are masters in this field, just as there are masters of portraiture and marine and historical themes. In fact flower artists have been gladdening the eyes of mankind from ancient Egyptian times to the present day.

Page 41

Paul CÉZANNE 1839–1906, French
"Still Life: Apples and Oranges"
Jeu de Paume Museum, Paris

A Provençal painter, Cézanne is one of the group of masters whose brilliant work forms the foundation of modern painting. His still lifes are almost architecturally composed. Everything is deliberately thought out with a view to its own worth and its relation to the whole. The very color contributes to the balanced effect, both in its selection and in the technique of its application. It emphasizes the folds of the cloth, shapes the general design, delineates the outlines, binds the different elements together.

Good craftsman that he was, Cézanne would return untiringly day after day to his canvas, refusing to leave the work until he was completely satisfied.

Page 42

Jean-Baptiste Siméon CHARDIN
1699–1779, French
"The Loaf"
Louvre, Paris

Chardin's colors spread over the canvas as if they really were composed of bread, flowers, china, and glass. The result is realistic, savory, and appetizing. In addition to still lifes Chardin painted domestic scenes with such titles as "The Grace" (before a meal), "Child with a Top", "The Rebuke" and a number of others.

STILL LIFE. The artist first arranges with great care the things he wants to paint, then sets to work to invest them with realism, poetry, or even mystery. Connoisseurs recognize definite groups of still life studies: pictures of things to eat, from Spain; pictures so lifelike you feel you must be looking at the real articles, from Italy; "vanities" such as a skull, a mirror, or a candle, from Flanders; and displays of sea foods, from Holland.

Page 43

Frans SNYDERS 1579–1657, Flemish
"A Fruit Seller"
Prado, Madrid

If you go to Antwerp, in Belgium, don't fail to visit Rubens' house; it was there, in a large studio now empty, that the enormous paintings were created which today adorn so many churches and museums.

To carry out these great undertakings the master surrounded himself with assistants, pupils, and practical admirers. To one of these, Frans Snyders, was assigned the task of painting the still lifes. You may be sure he was kept pretty busy, but sometimes he did find time to paint a picture of his own, such as this delightful collection of fruits and flowers.

Page 44

Pieter BRUEGHEL the Elder
1528–1569, Flemish
"Wedding Dance"
Detroit Institute of Arts, Michigan, USA

So much did he amuse those who knew him, this member of the Brueghel family was also known as Pieter the Comic. His studio generally turned out several copies of each of his works, which found their way into Europe's princely courts.

The best collection is at Vienna, where a whole salon is devoted to this artist. And what a vivid spot it is! A regular Flemish fair.

Page 45

David TENIERS the Younger 1610–1699, Flemish "The Village Fair"
Prado, Madro

The banners flutter in the breeze. People dance, drink, amuse themselves, quarrel. It's the day of the annual fête given by the local landowner, and everyone has been looking forward to it, one may safely guess, since the last one a year ago.

Teniers obviously enjoys telling us about this event, but the pleasure revealed in his work must not blind us to the deep thought he has put into the arrangement of the picture, both in layout and in blend of colors.

It is the same sort of story that Pieter Brueghel tells in his different manner.

Page 46

Jacob JORDAENS 1593–1678, Flemish
"The King Drinks" (part of a larger picture)
Royal Museum of Fine Arts, Brussels

The joy of living shines out of all these Flemish faces, concerned only with eating and drinking. Pushing and shoving, singing and getting drunk, are the order of the day.

Jordaens was one of the assistants (though not a pupil) in Rubens' painting "factory". There is a splendid picture by him, "The Riches of Autumn," in the Wallace Collection; the fruit and vegetables in the scene were painted by that other helper of Rubens, Frans Snyders.
Wallace Collection, London
Dulwich College Art Gallery, London

Page 47

Jan STEEN 1626–1679, Dutch
"The Feast of Saint Nicholas"
Rijksmuseum, Amsterdam

It is the Sixth of December; St. Nicholas and his toy-laden donkey have just passed, and the household is full of joy. The Dutch painters (the "Little Masters", as they came to be called) enjoyed depicting their homes, which were always carefully rearranged and lit for the purpose. But today is a fête day, and somewhat different—though in reality the apparent chaos is only another sort of rearrangement by the artist! People laugh and argue, the grown-ups annoy the children. . . .

Pages 48–49

Pieter BRUEGHEL the Elder 1528–1569, Flemish "Battle Between Carnival and Lent" (part of picture)

Carnival and Lent: each side has its procession, on one side the thin ones, on the other the fat. Chicken and pig's head on the spit, herrings on the oven ladle; a real tournament is about to begin. What fun they're having in this Flanders square! What a wealth of details you can pick out! The whole tableau seethes with life, energy, and comedy.

Page 50

Jerome (Hieronymus) BOSCH 1460–1516, Dutch
"The Conjurer"
Saint-Germain-en-Laye Museum, France

Bosch's pictures are extraordinary both in their subject matter and for his surrealistic way of treating it. For him everything is wrapped in mystery, symbolism, folklore; everything involves fairy tale, black magic, crazy invention.

Yet in this picture (an exception among his works) he has kept to normality—superficially at least. But has he really? While the conjurer does his trick, linger a little and study each figure attentively. What do you think?

Page 51

Louis Léopold BOILLY 1761–1845, French
"The Stage"
Cognacq-Jay Museum, Paris

The scene is picturesque and lively. It shows quite truthfully the sort of spectacle that the streets of former days provided for the passer-by. A party of tight-rope walkers have just set up their trestle stage, and one of them is addressing the public. The orchestra is playing. The trousered lady acrobat waits on her perch. The clown looks up at her.

Boilly paints each character with minute care, accurately recording every costume.

Pages 52–53

Each painter here has witnessed an ordinary scene and extracted from it what he considers to be the essence.

These two spirited pages will therefore give you a further opportunity to analyze and compare the various styles, which cover several centuries of painting.

Jean Tassel gives a straightforward account of the men operating the two-handed saw.

Vermeer and Courbet get rather more atmosphere into the women sifting corn and the girl making lace.

Gromaire shows his model crouched over his work.

The fish market furnishes the occasion for a fine still life.

Millet took a great interest in the peasants whose work and problems he placed on record.

The Van Gogh is an early example; he shows the weaver completely absorbed in his work.

Snyders once more betrays his delight in painting a Flemish fruit and flower market.

In France, Louis Le Nain has here made a studio out of the dark forge lit only by the blacksmith's fire.

Fernand Léger has caught a scene you can see for yourself wherever construction work is going on.

Jean TASSEL 1608–1667, French
 "The Carpenters"
 Château de Rohan, Strasbourg, France

Jan VERMEER van Delft 1632–1675, Dutch
 "The Lacemaker"
 Louvre, Paris

Gustave COURBET 1819–1877, French
 "The Winnowers"
 Nantes Museum, France

Marcel GROMAIRE Born 1892, French
 "The Flemish Reaper"
 Municipal Museum of Modern Art, Paris

Emmanuel DE WITTE 1617–1692, Dutch
 "Fish Market"
 Boymans-van Beuningen Museum, Rotterdam

Jean-François MILLET 1814–1875, French
 "The Gleaners"
 Louvre, Paris

Vincent VAN GOGH 1853–1890, Dutch
 "The Craft of Weaving"
 Kroller-Müller Foundation, Otterlo, Holland

Frans SNYDERS (attributed to) 1579–1657, Flemish
 "The Fruit-seller"
 Museum of Decorative Arts, Paris

Louis LE NAIN 1593–1648, French
 "The Forge"
 Louvre, Paris

Fernand LÉGER 1881–1955, French
 "The Builders"
 Fernand-Léger Museum, Biot, France

Page 54

Théodore GÉRICAULT 1791–1824, French
 "Light Cavalry Officer
 of the Imperial Guard on Horseback"
 Louvre, Paris

Géricault had two great interests, horses and painting. Thinking back to his childhood, he could see again the colorful officers of Napoleon's Empire, and he derived great pleasure from painting them.

UNDERPAINTING. Some painters, ever since early Renaissance days have worked on canvas suitably prepared to take paint, but left white. Others, however, especially in former times with older techniques, have preferred canvas "underpainted"—sometimes more than once—with various pale tints that give an added luster to the final colors applied on top.

Géricault favoured underpainting with a wash made from bitumen, a dark brown mineral substance; Poussin (a 17th-century French artist) treated his canvases with sepia, a brown pigment derived from the ink of the cuttlefish.
National Gallery, London

Page 55

Eugène DELACROIX 1798–1863, French
 "Knights in Combat in Open Country"
 Museum of Fine Arts, Boston, USA

Delacroix's life passed in an atmosphere of ordered calm that you would scarcely suspect from the passionate and stormy nature of his paintings and drawings!

His temperament is given full rein in this knightly combat;

the painting is meticulously planned, abounding in fury and violence, and beautifully coloured down to the last detail.
National Gallery, London
Wallace Collection, London

Pages 56–57
Greco-Roman Art: "Contest between Alexander and Darius"
Italy. Roman mosaic.
Before 1st cent. A.D.
National Museum, Naples

This great mosaic was the principal decoration of one of Pompeii's most beautiful houses. In 79 A.D. it disappeared under the lava and cinders from a severe eruption of Mount Vesuvius that buried the whole city for hundreds of years. It was rediscovered about 200 years ago, and at first everything that came to light was taken away, mostly to the National Museum at Naples, including this mosaic. But today you can wander through the excavated streets of ancient Pompeii and still see many fine mosaics and paintings in their original positions.

This picture—some of which is missing, of course—tells the story of the last battle between Alexander the Great and Darius, King of the Persians. It was probably copied from an earlier Greek painting.

MOSAICS. Into a bed of wet mortar or cement are set thousands of tiny colored squares of pottery, marble, glass, gold, etc. to reproduce a drawing made in advance. Mosaic art remained popular until fresco painting superseded it in the 13th century; today it is again finding fashion.

You may see Roman mosaics in Lullingstone (Kent), St. Albans, Rockbourne (Hampshire), and several other sites in England. The finest medieval mosaics are in Italy, Greece, Turkey, and Yugoslavia.

Pages 58–59
Paolo UCCELLO
1397–1475, Italian
"The Rout of San Romano" (part of picture)
National Gallery, London

The city of Florence was often at war with her neighbor Siena—but the battles were frequently more like ballets! They also inspired some fine paintings, in which the artists were able to show off their knowledge of the proper placing of the troops, the horses, the dying . . . And naturally the nobles, on such days of glory, took the opportunity to have their portraits made.

Uccello painted no fewer than four pictures of the Battle of San Romano. There was this one, now in the London National Gallery; another is now in the Louvre, a third in the Uffizi at Florence itself. The fourth vanished during a later war.
National Gallery, London
Ashmolean Museum, Oxford

Pages 60–61
Albrecht ALTDORFER
1480–1538, German
"Alexander in Battle at Arbela" (also called "Alexander's Victory")
Pinakothek Gallery, Munich, West Germany

Altdorfer, a strange character, painted his pictures in miniature; this famous battle scene (representing Alexander the Great's final victory over King Darius, in 331 B.C.) contains thousands of soldiers in quite a tiny space. The light is weird, the landscape looks bewitched. Indeed, Altdorfer was fascinated by landscapes; he painted several with no figures in them, centuries before any other artist would dream of such a thing.
Wernher collection, Luton Hoo, Bedfordshire

BATTLE PAINTINGS. To be a war artist carried much prestige, but all the work really took place in the calm of the studio, where the artist had leisure to compose a really worthwhile picture. The following are a few of the world's most celebrated battle scenes:

Piero della Francesca: "The Battle of the Milvius Bridge" (312 A.D. Roman Emperor Constantine defeats rival Maxentius). "Victory of Heraclius over Chosroes" (615 A.D.: Byzantine defeat of Persians) (*both in the Church of San Francesco, Arrezzo, Italy*).

Velasquez: "The Surrender of Breda" (by the Dutch to the Spaniards, 1625). (*Prado, Madrid.*)

Uccello: The three versions of the Rout of San Romano.

Goya: "The Second of May" (Massacre of Madrid citizens by Napoleon's Egyptian cavalry, 1808). (*Prado, Madrid*)

Antoine Jean Gros (1771–1835): "The Battlefield at Eylau" (Napoleon defeated Russians and Prussians, 1807). (*Louvre, Paris*)

Jacques Louis David (1748–1825): "Leonidas at Thermopylae" (pass where a handful of Greeks defied a huge Persian army in 480 B.C.). (*Louvre, Paris*)

Delacroix: "The Battle of Taillebourg" (Louis IX defeated Henry II of England, 1242). (*Versailles Museum, France*)

Picasso: "Guernica" (Spanish town bombed by Germans, 1936). (*Metropolitan Museum of Art, New York*)

The Imperial War Museum, London, contains a number of impressive paintings by Paul Nash (1889–1946, English) of battle scenes from the World War of 1914–1918.

Pages 62–63

Eugène ISABEY
1803–1886, French
"Jean Bart at the
Naval Battle of Texel"
Marine Museum, Paris

To be a marine artist is still an occupation that commands respect. Isabey, passionately devoted to history and to ships, was commissioned to paint this engagement, using research and his imagination; it was one of the many encounters of the French fleet during the reign of Louis XIV. The picture he evolved is today one of the treasures of the Maritime Museum. Texel is an island in the northern part of Holland.

Pages 64–65

William TURNER
1775–1851, English
"The Naval Battle of
Trafalgar"
Tate Gallery, London

Turner painted watercolors remarkable for their luminous and transparent effects. Dawn, noontide, dusk—he studied the light peculiar to each of them. And he was particularly interested in light over the sea.
Here, however, we have one of his pictures in which the play of light is not the most prominent feature. The ships jostle one another, the masts are broken, the tattered sails flap in the wind, the guns thunder; and one senses another drama in the tiny group at the base of the central mast: Admiral Nelson, victor in one of the greatest naval battles of all time, is about to die.

National Gallery, London
Tate Gallery, London (a fine collection)
British Museum, London

There are other Turner paintings in a great number of public collections throughout Great Britain.

Right:
Willem VAN DER VELDE the Younger
1633–1707, Dutch
"The Cannon Shot"
Rijksmuseum, Amsterdam

In every living room in Amsterdam, Leyden, or Delft one used to see on the walls a sea picture, a landscape featuring a frozen canal, and paintings extolling the glory of the Dutch Navy. Among the last-named, this example is the best known, and was copied countless times.

This artist, his father, and his brother were all painters; Willem and his father (Willem the Elder) were for many years Official Marine Artists in London, where they were the founders of British sea painting. Most of the sketches for their battle pictures were actually made during the thick of the fight!
National Maritime Museum, London (including many sketches)
Wallace Collection, London
National Gallery, London

Page 66

Antony VANDYCK (or VANDYKE)
1599–1641, Flemish
"Charles I of England"
Louvre, Paris

Van Dyck was a native of Antwerp, where he was apprenticed in a studio at the age of ten, later becoming a pupil and then chief assistant of Rubens. Later he went to England where, like Holbein in the previous century, he became Court Painter, changing the spelling of his name on receiving a knighthood and appearing as Sir Antony Vandyke.
He painted several portraits of Charles I, this being one of the finest. It shows the King out hunting on his palfrey, accompanied by his page. The colors are brilliant, the brushwork neat, the craftsmanship elegant. It is one of the most successful "official" portraits anywhere. Louis XV bought it during a sale and set it in the Louvre.

National Gallery, London
Wallace Collection, London

The Royal collection also contains a number of fine Vandykes, which are sometimes exhibited to the public.

Page 67

Jacques Louis DAVID 1748–1825, French
"The Coronation of Napoleon I"
Louvre, Paris

David was a fervent supporter of the French Revolution, and as a government Deputy voted for the execution of Louis XVI. Later he became an equally loyal supporter of Napoleon, who saw that he was not only a great artist but a clever propagandist. It was therefore natural for David to be appointed to paint the Coronation.
In the picture Napoleon has just been crowned, and in turn is crowning the Empress. She leans forward, while the Emperor's sisters help to carry the heavy cloak embroidered with gold bees. Pope Pius VII, who has come specially from Rome to Paris, gives his blessing. An absentee from the scene is Napoleon's mother, but she was present at the Louvre when the huge painting was exhibited there in 1807.

It took David and his pupils the intervening years (from December 1804) to complete his commission, which includes more than 100 portraits painted from life.

Pages 68–69

Benozzo GOZZOLI
1420–1497, Italian
"Procession of Princes"
Pitti Palace, Florence, Italy

The great Italian Medici family loved art in all its forms. Artists were always welcome at their court, and they filled their palaces with rare books, paintings, sculpture, and anything else they thought artistic. For the present picture, covering a wall of their private chapel, they commissioned Gozzoli, a pupil of the famous FRA ANGELICO (about 1400–1455), to show them journeying to Jerusalem in the guise of the Three Wise Men!
National Gallery, London (Gozzoli and Angelico)

Pages 70–71

Gentile DA FABRIANO
1370–1427, Italian
"The Adoration of the Magi"
Uffizzi Gallery, Florence, Italy

Here we have really seductive art, lavish, detailed, consisting entirely of foreground, sharply outlined, bright as jewelery, ornate and decorative as a Gothic tapestry.

We are back in the late Middle Ages, in a time when painters were often poets and musicians as well. Da Fabriano traveled about, telling the Gospel story in his pictures, from Venice to Florence, Brescia to Rome. And our eyes are gladdened by the sight of these sumptuously dressed personages, these Kings whose luxury is abandoned only at the Virgin's feet.

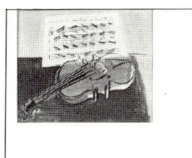

Page 72

Raoul DUFY 1877–1953, French
"The Red Violin"
National Museum of Modern Art, Paris

The brush has been used here for rapid sketching. The violin, realized by depicting just its essentials, is shown almost in monochrome (one color): a simple, artistic device at once delicate and powerful.

Dufy executed a whole series of paintings of this type, in honour of music, which he both loved and genuinely understood.

Homage to Mozart; the yellowish music stand and the red violin appear in several studies. This particular one was made at an interesting stage in Dufy's development, when he had just mastered his artistic style and seemed to be able to brush aside all difficulties. His work was on the road to enchantment.
Tate Gallery, London
Courtauld Institute, London

Page 73

Raoul DUFY 1877–1953, French
"Orchestra with Singer"
Louis Carré collection, Paris

Does Dufy make you feel here as though you were actually present at the concert? Certainly the scene appears almost audible as well as visible. Dufy was much influenced by the "Fauves" (see Illustrated Guide note to page 80 left), and you may find it interesting to compare his "wild" style with Matisse's.

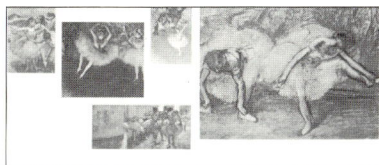

Pages 74–75

Edgar DEGAS
1834–1917, French
"Dancer in the Salmon Skirt"
"The Pas Battu" (in ballet, a high leap with rapid crossing and uncrossing of the feet in the air)
"Dancer behind the Scenes"
"Dancer on the Stage" (*Jeu de Paume Gallery, Paris*)
"Two Dancers" (*Niarchos collection*)

The first three pictures are all in the *Bührle collection, Zurich, Switzerland.*

Few people can long be interested in pictures without coming across Degas' ballet dancers. They leap, swerve, pirouette, rise on their toes, practice assiduously, bend double, fasten their sandals, make an entrance, curtsy before leaving the stage — and they do these things in all the important art galleries of the world.

Pictures that pulsate with life, always catching their subject at an unforeseen moment... Success in this kind of art requires lynx-eyed observation, a prodigious memory, immense skill, and the patience to make endless sketches, try-outs, roughs.

Pastel (see Illustrated Guide note to Page 13) is well suited to this rapid technique, since it serves as both pencil and means of soloring. Breaking with the tradition that all compositions must be built round a center, balanced, and carefully designed,

Degas' compositions were as hard to anticipate as they were original.

Degas is represented in most of the London galleries.

Page 76

Édouard VUILLARD 1868–1940, French
(The Imaginary Invalid)

Not all paintings are made for the purpose of showing in galleries or private houses. Some are put to the service of business or amusement, and if, on a visit to Paris, you get the chance to visit the Comedy Theatre of the Champs Élysées, you will find this scene from one of the most famous plays by one of France's greatest dramatists, Molière (1622–1673), in the foyer.

THE DECORATOR'S ART. Often today—just as in earlier periods—an artist is asked to paint a "mural", in other words to decorate a wall in a theatre, public building, or office block. The task involves quite different considerations from those governing a picture enclosed in a movable frame. The painter has to think of the relationship of his picture to the rest of the building; it must harmonize with the style of architecture, and not be out-of-key with the purpose of the place.

Vuillard decorated such notable buildings as the Palais de Chaillot, Paris, and the League of Nations Building at Geneva.

Paintings: *Tate Gallery, London. Courtauld Institute, London*

Page 77

Georges SEURAT 1859–1891, French
"The Circus"
Jeu de Paume Gallery, Paris

Paint lots of little yellow dots and blue dots jumbled together, step back, and the color you see is green. You have created an "optical mixture". This was the method Seurat adopted for his patiently built pictures. From a distance their subjects spring into startling life, and whether they are landscapes, interiors, or portraits, become infused with wonderful atmosphere and color.

POINTILLISM. The 'dot' technique. This technique is also called Neo-Impressionist, because the artists who used it were bent on carrying Impressionism—the style developed by Monet, Cézanne, Renoir and others—a stage further. Pointillism may be called midway between Impressionism and Cubism (see Illustrated Guide note to pages 78–79 right).

National Gallery, London
Tate Gallery, London
Courtauld Institute, London

Pages 78–79

Left:
Henri de
TOULOUSE-LAUTREC
1864–1901, French
"The Jockey"
Colored lithograph
National Library, Paris

Master of both drawing and painting, and the creator of poster art, Toulouse-Lautrec was equally at home with lithography (see Illustrated Guide note to page 24). His visual memory was astonishing. This lithograph has all the vividness of a lightning drawing: horse and jockey have been seized at a single instant, as in a camera snapshot. You can almost feel the horse move.

The biggest collection is at the artist's birthplace, Albi, France.
Tate Gallery, London
Courtauld Institute, London—and a number of other British galleries

Center;
André LHOTE 1885–1962, French
"Rugby"
National Museum of Modern Art, Paris

You need to have watched a rugger match, with its straining scrums, its sudden rushes, its tackles, the winged feet of a three-quarter, to share the artist's feeling for the game as here expressed. Technically, the colors are laid on in simplified and stylized patterns, and the design in the form of a pyramid is meant to follow the distribution of players on the field.

Right:
Robert DELAUNAY 1885–1941, French
"The Runners"
Madame Delaunay's collection, Paris

Everything here is geometrical, and yet there is suppleness and movement throughout. The runners who bear down upon us are placed in the picture with great precision and move with a harmonious rhythm. To extract what he felt were the essentials of the scene, the artist studied it with a close attention that left it clearly imprinted on his memory.

CUBISM. Cubism may be traced back to Cézanne, though its first real exponents were Picasso and Georges Braque (born 1882); it was a breakaway from Impressionism, abandoning surface impressions in favor of considering every object in all three dimensions—as though you could see all around it at once. The cubists also reacted against the innumerable brush strokes of Impressionism by depicting everything in terms of large cubes, cones, and cylinders.

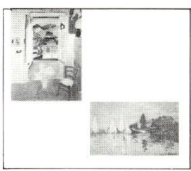

Page 80

Left:
Henri MATISSE 1869–1954, French
"Open Window at Colliloure"
Bührle collection, Zurich, Switzerland

Here is the sort of gay and happy window that makes you think of summer holidays. The sunlight floods into the room, the countryside invites a stroll—and yet the painter seems to have been reluctant to show us this moment of truth.

Each feature of the picture is hastily suggested. The colors are not the real colors of the objects they depict, but colors imagined and idealized. The canvas is bare in parts; a few lines conjure up a pot of flowers; reds, blues, and yellows are laid on just as they came from the tubes, unmixed; shadows are non-existent.

FAUVISM. "Les Fauves"—"The Wild Beasts"—was the name given by a critic in 1905 to a group of artists whose works were all showing in the same Paris salon and all, in their various styles, displaying the rough, unfinished characteristics you see in this Matisse. He himself (the principal "Fauve") said: "The purpose of colors is to invest what we see with the power to shock our senses." With their violent tones, their disconcerting novelty, and their revolutionary nature, it is small wonder that the "wild beast" epithet stuck to these artists.

Right:

Claude MONET 1840–1926, French
"Yachts at Argenteuil"
Jeu de Paume Gallery, Paris

An airy, fresh, transparent painting this. The light plays over the yachts, reflecting them in the water; the wind bellies and twists the sails; and Monet captured the atmosphere of it all by doing something very new and bold; he painted the picture in its entirety from a small boat, instead of making a sketch and working on it later in his studio. This was the beginning of Impressionism (see Illustrated Guide note to page 85).

Page 81

Raoul DUFY 1877–1953, French
"Riders in a Wood"
National Museum of Modern Art, Paris
(gift of Mme. Raoul Dufy)

Dufy is an artist whose canvases, as we have already seen, are easily recognized: a few pure colors skilfully applied, combined with free, evocative drawing suggesting high-speed work. The result is landscapes in which you seem to smell the perfumes, countrysides humming with insects, skies criss-crossed by the flight of birds . . . and woods through which riders pass.

(see note to page 72 for Dufy pictures on view in Great Britain)

Page 82

Above:
John CONSTABLE 1776–1837, English
"Dedham Mill"
Victoria and Albert Museum, London

Landscape occupies a place of major importance in the history of English art.

Constable used the inspiration of nature to produce dazzling sketches that captivate and enchant us. He said he wished them to "sparkle with the dew like the trees, bushes, and grass of the real world when it is bathed in light."

Afterwards, in the studio, he would use his sketches to compose large pictures in which he tried to express everything unpredictable and fleeting in the atmosphere of the English countryside.

Victoria and Albert Museum (the largest collection). Most other London and several provincial galleries

Below:
Jean-Baptiste Camille COROT 1796–1875, French
"Florence from the Boboli Gardens"

It is towards the end of the afternoon that the countryside attains its truest artistic values and its most characteristic colors. This is the time that in France they used to call "Corot's hour".

In this scene we are in old Florence, or rather on the edge of it, where the terrace of the Boboli Gardens dominates the city. Beyond the cypresses appear the Cathedral, the Campanile, the Church of Santa Croce, and, roseate in the distance, the hill of Fiesole.

Few artists have been more often credited with the work of imitators, and the victim of deliberate forgeries. Nevertheless, his genuine output was large, and his paintings appear in many British galleries. There is no one preeminent collection.

Page 83

Left:
Paul GAUGUIN 1848–1903, French
"Riders on the Sands at Tahiti"
Niarchos collection

Gauguin said that each time an artist discovered a color tone he should exploit it to the utmost. Hence the sumptuous rose-colored sands, the blues, the greens, the intense reds, the sudden bursts of yellow, in this scene.

Away with projected shadows, with perspective, with differentiation between various substances. The painter's eye recalls only blobs that move and form colored silhouettes.
Tate Gallery, London
Courtauld Institute, London
National Gallery, Edinburgh
City Museum, Manchester

Right:
WANG-Meng c. 1308–1385 (Yuan Dynasty), Chinese
"Mountain in Autumn"
National Museum of the Chinese People's Republic, Peking

In most Chinese pictures (other than those on vases or ivory, or lacquer work) colored inks replace paints, a roll of silk or rice paper takes the place of canvas. Chinese landscapes are never intended to represent "real" scenes; every object shown has a symbolic as well as a natural significance for the Oriental viewer, who can "read" the deeper meaning in a tree or mountain as few of us can. But we can appreciate the spiritual quality that this double purpose gives to Chinese paintings.
Chinese paintings: *British Museum, London*

Page 84
Henri ROUSSEAU ("Douanier Rousseau")
1844–1910, French
"Old Juniet's Trap"
Orangery Museum, The Tuileries, Paris

New styles in art have always excited laughter and jeers among the ignorant, but few painters have endured quite so much of it as Rousseau. Because he continued in his full-time job as a customs official he was contemptuously dismissed as a "Sunday painter". But he refused to be discouraged, and went on painting to please himself and his friends.

Without leaving his studio he conjured up jungle scenes with terrible battles involving roaring lions; leopards about to leap; snakes and crocodiles. Or, in contrast, he dreamed of starlit nights in the desert. He drew inspiration from gun catalogues, hunting brochures, even picture-postcards.

Page 85
Camille PISSARRO 1830–1903
"Approach to the Village"
Jeu de Paume Gallery, Paris

Looking everyone's idea of a painter, with broad-brimmed hat, pipe, and the beard of an Old Testament prophet, carrying easel, palette, and paint box, Pissarro—part French, part Negro, part Portuguese-Jewish—would install himself at his chosen spot, in this case the verge of the road leading into the village of Voisins, near Paris.

He applied his colors in tiny dabs, building up a scene notable for its firm construction that nevertheless allows a sense of mellow softness, of "spring in the air". Pissarro is one of the greatest of the group known as the Impressionists.

IMPRESSIONISM. Monet, Alfred Sisley, Pissarro, Cézanne, Degas, Renoir, and—all too rare in the art world—two women, Mary Cassatt and Berthe Morisot: these were the most noted of the Impressionists. Their great preoccupation was with *light,* the play of light on every object, from a landscape to a face. This, they reasoned, was what governed the impression received by the eye, and this was what they tried to reproduce by their by the eye, and this was what they tried to reproduce by their use of tiny brush strokes, avoidance of rigid outlines, and by painting the whole picture (like Monet's yachts) on the spot instead of finishing it in the studio.

Pissarro is another artist whose work is to be found in most of our important galleries.

Page 86
Marc CHAGALL Born 1887
Russian: Paris school of artists.
"The Reclining Poet"
Tate Gallery, London

A painting by Chagall is like a mixture of reality and fairy tale. The color is closely bound up with the constantly adventurous drawing. People float on air, a cockerel suggests the winged horse Pegasus, a donkey plays the violin and flowers swoon with love. . . .

Like Vuillard, Chagall (a Russian by birth) is also a noted decorator, particularly in the theatre. The remarkable ceiling of the Paris Opera is his work.
Tate Gallery, London

 Page 87

Henri MATISSE 1869–1954, French
"The King's Sorrow"
National Museum of Modern Art, Paris

"A picture on a wall should be like a bunch of flowers in a room", Matisse once said. And in the closing years of his life, as if returning to a childhood pleasure, he composed his most beautiful works from scraps of paper cut out and stuck on a mount—a technique known as "Collage", from the French *coller*, to stick.

COLLAGE. Cloth, thin wood, and other materials are occasionally used as well as, or instead of, paper. The materials may be stuck on to the canvas or board background to form the whole picture or only part of it, combined with painting; and sometimes they themselves are overpainted.

The largest collection of Matisse pictures is in Moscow.

 Page 88

Pierre-Auguste RENOIR 1841–1919, French
"Jean Renoir Drawing"
Privately owned

Here is young Jean, pencil in hand, posing for his father in the latter's celebrated studio at his home, "Collettes", in the Alpine village of Cagnes overlooking the French Riviera. You may think he looks less like a model than a boy learning to be an artist himself; and so he was, of another kind, for he grew up to become a world-famous (and highly artistic) film director.

There were three boys in the Renoir family, and their likenesses are to be seen in many galleries; yet Auguste Renoir is even better known for his paintings of girls and young women—and for his exquisite, highly individual treatment of trees and flowers.

National Gallery, London
Tate Gallery, London
Courtauld Institute, London

INDEX

Altdorfer, A., 60, 101
American painting, 31, 34, 95–6
Asia Minor toys, 26, 94
Audubon, 4–5, 91

Boilly, L.-L., 50, 99
Bonnard, P., 39, 97
Bosch, H., 50, 99
Brueghel, J., 40, 98
Brueghel, P., 44, 48–9, 98–9

Cassatt, M., 31, 95
Cezanne, P., 41, 98
Chagall, M., 86, 106
Chardin, J.-B. S., 42, 98
Chinese drawing, 18, 92
  painting, 21, 83, 93, 106
Chi Pai Shih, 18
Clouet, J., 32, 96
Constable, J., 82, 105
Corot, J.-B. C., 82, 105
Courbet, G., 52, 100
Cranach, L., 30, 95

David, J.-L., 67, 102
Degas, E., 74–5, 103
Delacroix, E., 24, 94
De la Tour, G., 37, 97
Delaunay, R., 79, 104
Delvitte, E., 53, 100
Drawing, Chinese, 18, 93
  Dutch, 25, 94
  Italian, 20, 93
  Japanese, 14, 92
Dufy, R., 72–3, 81, 103, 105
Durer, A., 12, 92
Dutch drawing, 25, 94
Dutch painting, 28, 32, 50, 52–3, 65, 94, 96, 98–9, 100, 102

Egyptian painting, 8, 91
  pottery, 17, 92
  toys, 26, 93
English painting, 34, 65, 82, 96, 98, 102, 105

Fabriano, G. Da, 70–1, 103
Flemish painting, 30, 36, 40, 44, 46, 48–9, 53, 66, 95–6, 98–9, 100, 102
French lithographs, 24, 94
  painting, 28, 37, 38, 42, 50, 52, 54, 62–3, 72–88, 94, 97, 98–100, 102–7
  tapestry, 11, 92

Gainsborough, Thos., 34, 96, 98
Gauguin, 83, 105–6
Gericault, T., 54, 100
German painting, 12, 30, 60, 92, 95
Gogh, V. van, 53, 100
Goya, F. J. de, 30, 95
Gozzoli, B., 68–9, 103
Greco-Roman Art, 56–7, 101
Greek toys, 26, 94
Gromaire, M., 52, 100

Hokusai, K., 14–15, 92

Indian painting, 22, 94
  toys, 26, 94
Isabey, E., 62–3, 102
Italian drawing, 20, 93
  painting, 31, 58–9, 68–71, 95, 101, 103

Japanese painting, 9, 91
  prints, 14–15, 37, 92, 97
  toys, 26, 94
Jordaens, J., 46, 99

Katsushika Hokusai, 14–15, 92

Lascaux, 6, 91
Leger, F., 53, 100
Le Nain, L., 28, 53, 94, 100

Lhote, A., 79, 104
Lithography, 24, 94

Ma Lin, 21, 93
Manet, E., 38, 97
Matisse, 80, 87, 105, 107
Mexican pottery, 16, 92
Millet, J.-F., 53, 100
Miniatures, Persian, 23, 94
Modigliani, 31, 96
Monet, C., 38, 80, 97, 105
Mori Sosen, 9, 91
Moro, A., 32, 96
Mosaics, 56–7, 101

Painting, American, 31, 95–6
  Chinese, 21, 83, 93, 106
  Dutch, 28, 32, 50, 52–3, 65, 94, 96, 98–100, 102
  Egyptian, 8, 91
  English, 34, 65, 82, 96, 98, 102, 105 105
  Flemish, 30, 36, 40, 44, 46, 48–9, 53, 66, 95–6, 98–9, 100, 102
  French, 28, 37, 38, 42, 50, 52, 54, 62–3, 72–88, 94, 97–100, 102–7
  German, 12, 30, 60–1, 92, 95
  Indian, 22, 94
  Italian, 31, 58–60, 68–70, 95, 101, 103
  Japanese, 9, 91
  Persian, 23, 94
  Prehistoric, 6, 91
  Spanish, 13, 30–1, 92, 95, 96
Persian miniatures, 23, 94
  painting, 94
Peruvian pottery, 19, 92
Picasso, P., 13, 31, 92, 95
Pisanello, A., 20, 92
Pissarro, 85, 106
Pottery, Mexican, 16, 92
  Peruvian, 19, 92

Prints, Japanese, 14, 15, 92

Rembrandt, Van Rijn, 25, 94
Renoir, P.-A., 89, 107
Reynolds, Sir J., 96
Rousseau, H., 84, 86, 106
Rubens, P.P., 30, 95

Sosen, 9, 91
Snyders, Fr., 43, 53, 98, 100
Steen, J., 46, 99
Seurat, G., 77, 104

Tassel, 52, 100
Teniers, D., 45, 99
Toulouse-Lautrec, H. de, 78–9, 104
Toys, Asia Minor, 26, 94
  Egypt, 26, 94
  Greece, 26, 94
  India, 26, 94
  Japan, 26, 94
  Norway, 26, 94
Turner, Wm., 64–5, 102

Uccello, 58–9, 101
Utamaro, K., 37, 97

Van Der Velde, W., 65, 102
Vandyck, A., 66, 102
Velasquez, D.R., 33, 96
Vermeer, J., 28, 94
Vos, Marten de, 36, 97
Vuillard, E., 76, 104

Wang-Meng, 83, 106
Whistler, Jas., 35, 96
Witte, E. de, 53, 100

Printed in West-Germany by Mohn & Co GmbH, Gütersloh